My Life's Journey with The Lord

Amara Ugo

Table of Contents

Title page……………………………………………… 1

Table of Contents………………………………………… 2

Preface………………………………………………….3

Acknowledgements………………………………… 6

Chapter 1 – A bit of background…………………….7

Chapter 2 – How it all began……………………….10

Chapter 3 – God amid it all…………………………16

Chapter 4 – Weaning me off human dependence ……………………………………………………….26

Chapter 5 - The most important decision………….35

Chapter 6 – More things I have learnt over the years……………………………………………….44

Preface

Over the years, I have come to realize that our lives are not random. Often, we assume that things happen either by coincidence, fate, hard work, principles, or other factors. While some of these may play a role, I believe that ultimately, our lives are predestined in Christ. The family we come from, the nation we are part of, our gifts, and areas of strength all have a purpose. The Bible states in Jeremiah 1:5, "Before I formed you in the womb, I knew you; before you were born, I set you apart; I appointed you as a prophet to the nations".

God has a purpose for each of us, as His children, and to fully comprehend and align with this purpose, we need to deepen our relationship with Him. Having close intimacy with God helps us learn His heart and understand the intention behind our existence. There is no fulfilment of purpose outside of Christ. People may argue that unbelievers appear to achieve and thrive in many things. This may be true however, there is no real achievement as Christians, if we do not fulfil our purpose on earth as ordained by God.

I have been on a journey with the Lord over these past years, learning and understanding my purpose and how the circumstances of my life can come together for good. Having been born again for over a decade, I thought my relationship with God at that time was sufficient, but God is revealing to me that there is so much more.

I have started to learn the true meaning of trusting in the Lord with ALL my heart. Many of us are familiar with the verse that says, "Trust in the Lord with all your heart and lean not on your own understanding" (Proverbs 3:5). But how many of us truly grasp what this means and are willing to practice it? We live in a world that relies heavily on our physical senses—what we see, hear, touch, and feel. Thus, trusting our instincts seems 'normal' in a physical world.

There is also a drive in culture to be self-reliant and self-confident. Yet, the Bible encourages us to do just the opposite—to refrain from trusting our own understanding and put ALL our trust in Him. Throughout this learning process, God has exposed idols within my heart that I unknowingly clung to, hindering my ability to trust Him fully. As these idols were exposed and dealt with, I began to experience true dependence on God, resulting in a relationship and intimacy with Christ that allow me to hear Him clearly.

I now understand that my existence is not random; my placement on this earth was predestined. His guidance and direction propel me daily toward fulfilling His will on earth, as it is in heaven. As you read this book, I pray, as Paul did in Ephesians 1:18-21, that the eyes of your understanding will be enlightened to know the hope of His calling, to grasp how you are His glorious inheritance, and to continually experience the power He made available to you through faith in Jesus' name. Amen!

Acknowledgement

I want to give all glory to Almighty God for His guidance, direction, and wisdom throughout the process of writing this piece. I recognize that writing this would not have been possible without Him.

A special thank you to my brother, Ikenna, for his encouraging feedback and support while reviewing the draft.

Lastly, I want to express my heartfelt gratitude to my husband for his unwavering love, encouragement, and support which have been instrumental in this process. I am truly grateful for your support.

Chapter 1

A bit of background

Life as I knew it growing up felt easy. My parents had six children, and I am the only girl among five brothers. Although now I understand that it was not always easy for my parents to cater to all of us, at the time, I was shielded from the difficulties. As an only girl, I was not overly pampered, and my parents ensured I learned how to take care of the home. I learned the duties of a female in a typical Eastern Nigerian household. We are a close-knit family, and I felt that most of the things I needed were provided.

Growing up, I noticed an unusual grace around me. Things that might be difficult for others would somehow seem to come easily to me. For instance, I am not one to study for hours for an exam. So long as I attended classes, during exam periods, I only need to scan through my notes before the exams and I will ace them. My roommate during my university days would move in with other students so that she could study for exams. She made a statement that after playing around with me during exam periods, when results are published, I will have As or Bs, and she will not do so well. Even at the end of my university education, the head of the department on the day the results were being given out wondered aloud how I was able to come out with such a good result, and he had never heard of me.

A similar situation happened when I graduated and was looking for employment. A friend submitted my CV after I had had several attempts and had given up. I got the banking job even though it was not related to what I studied. I thrived in the field and enjoyed the employment until I left Nigeria to join my husband in the UK. One of my elder brothers would always call me 'the favoured one'. There were countless times when God saved me from serious harm during my university days and while working in Nigeria. These are some of the many examples of God's grace and favour around me growing up. Everything seemed to be working well for me, and I did not struggle to get anything I needed.

My mother is a very spiritual woman and has a close relationship with God. When I was finishing up with my secondary education, she introduced me and my siblings to having a covenant time with the Lord, where you choose an hour in the day and spend it quietly in God's presence. This entailed going into a quiet room, praying, worshipping, and reading the bible or some selected Christian books that helped us to learn more about God. Initially, my siblings and I found this very tasking and did not understand why we needed to do this. We would often sleep off during our covenant time, or we would not go in at all, but my mother would keep checking in to make sure we were doing the right thing. Little did I know that this covenant time, which builds intimacy with God, would literally save my life.

Chapter 2

How it all began

After my university education and completing my National Youth Service Corps (NYSC), I connected with my husband through my eldest brother. We got married a couple of years later, and the following year after our marriage, I joined him in the UK. As I stated in the previous chapter, everything seemed to work out when it concerned me, and I was very happy with how things were going so far. Three months after joining my husband in the UK, I got pregnant, and that was the beginning of the troubles.

The first three months of the pregnancy were difficult due to morning sickness and other minor issues. When the baby was due, I had a traumatic experience during childbirth. I had a C-section and a few weeks afterwards, went back into theatre due to internal bleeding. Eventually, I healed, and we looked forward to raising our son. As our first son grew up, we noticed that he was delayed in speech, he was hyperactive and did not seem to be acting like his peers. This was very confusing. The difficulty was compounded by the fact that I was in a new country. I was trying to learn another culture, which is very different from mine, and I was away from the comfort of home. Initially, my husband and I felt that it was just a phase that he would outgrow in a few years and by three years of age, he would have picked up. However, that was not the case, and as he clocked three years old, he was diagnosed with autism and global developmental delay.

I had never heard the word autism until my first son got the diagnosis. My feelings at that point were indescribable, and to date, I still struggle to adequately articulate how I felt when I researched this condition. I did not understand what was happening. Usually, there is a family history or traumatic experience for the child during their birth that causes autism. However, there was no apparent cause of autism in our case. The doctors said that it could be a genetic mutation because nobody in our family history had autism. We were told there is no cure. That it is a lifelong condition, and depending on where the child is on the spectrum, he may or may not have a somewhat normal life. I was shattered. My life had been wonderful till this point, and nothing had hit me as hard as this before. Thankfully, I had built some intimacy with God at this point by spending time in His presence daily. And now every time I went to God's presence, I was crying and asking God questions. I could not understand what was happening.

I took in again. My second child was another lovely boy. After a few months, we noticed that he was not putting on weight because he was always throwing up all his food and was not retaining enough. Another diagnosis – reflux! I thought, here we go again. As doctors advised, he was fitted with an NG-tube in his nose so that they could pass milk through his nose to his stomach. This was supposed to ensure that the food stays in his stomach and he does not keep throwing up, as he would when he eats with his mouth. This was a short-term plan to be reviewed and mouth feeding reintroduced when things settle. Our son ended up having the NG tube for 12 months. At the end of the twelve months, doctors advised that he should have surgery and have the tube placed in his stomach because he still needed support with his feeding. The NG tube on his face was causing him bruises every time the tapes were removed. We agreed with the doctors as we did not feel there was any other option. Our son had this tube in his stomach for over 5 years. Throughout this period, he was not eating anything by mouth. With the difficulties with eating, we also noticed that he had similar delays as his elder brother. He was not speaking yet, and although not hyperactive, he was not meeting his developmental milestones either. It was a very difficult time, and I felt like God had abandoned us.

My third child came five years later, another gorgeous boy. His birth was a miracle because there were some complications during conception, but God intervened and saved us. As he grew up, we again began to see some of the difficulties we saw in his brothers. He had delayed speech, was hyperactive and was not meeting his milestones. I am naturally a laid-back and reserved person. However, the issues and difficulties that my children were experiencing meant that before they were enrolled in any school, I would meet with the head of the school, along with other key staff, to ensure that the right support was in place before they started school. Some of my experiences with schools were horrible and heartbreaking. The way they would describe the children and refuse to have them enrolled in their school broke my heart repeatedly. Although as I learnt more about the way the system worked, I understood my rights to advocate appropriately for my children.

People who have not seen or gone through similar experiences may not understand what this can do to a family. The situation we were facing meant that we could not have proper discussions with our children. If they are hurt, they could not say what exactly happened. We could not act like other families who have discussions about different things. I love children and have always looked forward to the amazing relationship I would have with mine. How they would not be able to keep secrets from me because we would be very close and talk about everything. I had imagined dinner table discussions, and now it was not the case. It made me feel like I had failed as a parent because I could not properly understand my children enough to keep them as safe as I wanted to.

Another aspect of this is their involvement with other children. Some activities that are done in the schools, for instance, sports days, nativity plays, and such days, are days to come extra prepared. This is because on these days, my children are not able to participate in what others are doing. Most times, the school attempts to involve them, which can be so difficult. All the other families are looking on while you are out there trying to support your child to at least sit with others, but they would not and most times I ended up taking them out of the activity. The heartache and shame can be unbearable at times. We wondered what is going on? Are we cursed? Can God not see this? Is there no balm in Gilead? We have been praying and believing God to heal our children, but days have become months and months have become years, yet we are still here.

Chapter 3

God amid it all

The bible says in Romans 8:28, "And we know that all things work together for good for those who love the Lord, who are called according to his purpose." I struggled to understand how the above chapter was true and how God could possibly cause the chaos in our home to work for my good. In my eyes, things were falling apart. My children were not looking like the promises of God. There were illnesses, delays, sorrow, heartache, and much worry. However, God in His mercy kept me and my husband from falling into serious depression, deadly illnesses, or worse, death.

People often wondered how I was still able to smile and carry on with life, given the difficulties we were facing. Others said that we do not look like what we are going through. However, I know that God gives divine strength and enablement to us when we ask Him to do that which may seem impossible to do on our own. God held my heart and preserved us throughout the early years of our children's difficulties. It was the most trying time of my life, but I felt strengthened to carry on doing what I needed to do. God continued to work in the background to draw me closer in intimacy with Him.

At this time, although I was keeping my covenant time, I was not growing in intimacy and maturity in Christ. A ten-year-old child does not remain the same in growth, development, and maturity throughout the period from one year to ten years. I have been born again for over ten years at this time, but there was no visible sign that I was growing and maturing. I was not hearing clear and direct instructions from God because I still depended on my mother to interpret most of my dreams. This is not to dispute the importance of being guided and discipled; however, it is to state that God expects us to grow. The bible says in Hebrews 5:12, "For though by this time you ought to be teachers, you need someone to teach you again the basic principles of the oracles of God. You need milk, not solid food!".

It seemed like part of the reason I was not completely focused on God and growing in Him was because I had faith in the people and structures around me. The bible says in Jeremiah 17:9-10, "The heart is hopelessly dark and deceitful, a puzzle that no one can figure out. But I, GOD, search the heart and examine the mind. I get to the heart of the human. I get to the root of things. I treat them as they really are, not as they pretend to be." At the time, I was unaware that although I prayed and believed that I trusted in God, this was not entirely true. I did trust in God, but I also trusted that the people around me and the structures within the UK where I live would bring the solutions to the issues we were experiencing. However, the bible says in Proverbs 3:5, "Trust in the LORD with all thine heart; and lean not unto thine own understanding." The first part of this verse says, Trust in the Lord with ALL your heart, not some of your heart. This was where I was getting it wrong. I needed to learn to trust God with everything and in everything, instead of trusting in anything or anyone else. God, in His mercy, began to wean me off everything!

Weaning me off trusting systems and structures

Hospital/Science

As previously stated, I was born in Nigeria and therefore experienced the health system in Nigeria. As I currently live in the UK and have compared both systems, it seems natural that I would be thrilled that I now have access to the UK health system. I was certain that any health issues we would ever have would easily be solved because of our location. But I was missing it. As children of God, our trust should be in God, not in a place or thing. The bible tells us to be spiritually minded (Romans 8:6) and not to conform to the patterns of this world (Romans 12:2). This means that in all things, we should ensure that we are walking in line with the will of God, with our eyes focused and trusted in Him alone.

The world may trust in science and health systems for healing, but we should trust in the Lord for our healing. He might decide to use the health systems or any other means He chooses, but our trust should be in Him, not the systems. There are many places in the bible where God speaks about our health. For example, the bible says in the ending part of Exodus 15:26, "I am the Lord your healer. Jeremiah 33:6 says, "I will bring health and healing to it, I will heal my people and will let them enjoy abundant peace and security". Therefore, we ought to go to God when we have ANY challenges and trust His guidance.

However, I was still in the process of learning the above. As time passed, I began to see the flaws in the health system that I had trusted so much.

There were no solutions to the issues our children were facing; instead, our experience showed that in some cases, the system seemed to work against us. For example, we kept pushing to get support for our second son so that he could start learning to eat with his mouth. He had been tube-fed for many years and was now food-averse.

This was completely refuted with excuses about it not being the right time, but instead, we were provided free equipment and milk to continue feeding him through his tube. This continued for over five years. However, this is not to say that the health system is not doing an amazing job. It is just to state that things were not working for us because we had not learnt as children of God to go to God first and trust His process. The bible says in Psalm 37:5-7, "Commit thy way unto the LORD; Trust also in him; And he shall bring it to pass". This means to present everything to Him first.

I eventually learnt to present everything to God, and we continued praying for God to make a way. God started showing different family members and friends in dreams where my son was eating with his mouth. He showed my immediate elder brother, my co-wife, my sister-in-law, one of my close friends, and then He showed me.

At the appointed time, a family friend came to visit us with his girlfriend. During the visit, the lady asked what was wrong with our son and whether any conditions were preventing him from eating with his mouth. At this time, nothing physically was preventing him from eating with his mouth except fear, because he had become food-averse due to not eating with his mouth for years.

After the visit, the lady later told me that she became restless and started searching for a solution. She found a clinic in another country where children with similar difficulties are taught to eat without a tube. As I had learnt to pray about everything, we began to present it to God, and that was how my family travelled to this country to attend the two-week intensive therapy. Thankfully, God restored our son's ability to eat at that clinic. We knew that God did this because some families had visited the clinic multiple times before their child started eating, and for other families, their children did not learn to eat with their mouths after the therapies. But God, in His mercy, did the miracle for us.

Another profound way that God confirmed that this was Him was when the lady who told us about this clinic contacted me after we returned to the

UK. During our discussion, she said that it was God who had caused us to meet. She shared that after directing us to the clinic, her relationship with our family friend broke down. To her, the whole relationship was orchestrated by God so that she would guide us to the clinic for our son to get his healing.

This experience taught me that God can choose to work in different ways, as the bible says, God's ways are not our ways and His thoughts are not our thoughts (Isaiah 55:8). I was trusting that the health system would provide the solution to my son's feeding issues instead of trusting God to work out His miracle. God can choose to use science or any other system to bring us freedom, but my trust must be in Him. I have learnt that no matter what, my first response is to present it to God and trust Him. I will follow whichever direction He chooses to take me through because in Him is life and everything I would ever need.

The school system

The next was the education system. I had previously anticipated that my children would have a wonderful experience schooling in the UK. It was not an area I had any worries about whatsoever; however, that did not turn out to be the case. Due to the difficulties our children were having, I experienced another side of the education system in the UK, which many families may not know.

As I had stated previously, enrolling my children in some schools caused some traumatic experiences that I would not wish anyone else to experience. It started with my first son, who we noticed had hyperactive behaviour and delayed speech while in preschool. As he was ready to be enrolled in nursery school, some of the schools near our home at the time refused to have him enrolled in their school. At this time, I was still trying to understand what was happening with him and desperately needed support from the school to work with me in helping him learn.

One of the schools outrightly said no, that he cannot be part of their school, even when other professionals were offering to provide support.

This marked the beginning of my journey with the school system. I quickly understood that the expectations I had about the support I would receive from schools were not going to be met. Probably because I had most of my education in Nigeria, I had a perception of how the education system should be. Our experience of the children attending a normal school was difficult.

It felt as if our son cried, screamed, jumped, or did anything outside of the norm in school, you are called to pick him up. I wondered how this was supposed to help him learn when he does not spend sufficient time in school. I was then advised to try a special school because apparently, the staff are more equipped to deal with any challenges. I agreed because we were just looking for solutions. That turned out to be another negative experience as well. The children were cared for, but the expectation around their educational attainment was low. You will hear things like "your child is not ready yet" or "he is doing amazing" when he is seriously lagging in those areas. I did not see the daily practice and learning that would support the children to learn in the areas where they needed it.

We also witnessed a high staff turnover within the special schools, which meant that today you have this teacher and next time there is a different teacher in the class; therefore, there is no continuity of learning for the child. I believe that this was why it seemed like their curriculum was being repeated. They seemed to be learning the same things year after year.

This is not to criticise the system because an average person's experience may be more positive, but due to the difficulties of our children, our experience was a huge disappointment with the system. I was constantly having to chase after the teachers to know what they were doing with the children. My three children were in three different schools, both mainstream and special schools, but there were not many positive results from any of them as time passed. I was completely devastated. Once again, my trust and expectations in the system have not gone as I had anticipated.

Chapter 4

Weaning me off human dependence

The process of weaning continued. The first person that God weaned me from dependence on was my lovely husband. My husband is my closest friend and can be so dependable that at times you forget that he is human – and therefore can fail. We have a beautiful friendship, relationship, and everything in between. I feel truly blessed by God for giving me such a wonderful man as my spouse. However, as the difficulties with our children began, we could not understand what was going on.

I would often try to seek comfort and reassurance from my husband; however, he was trying to process what was happening as well. He could not provide the solution to our dilemma as he usually would have. Instead, he was becoming broken with the situation. His vision of having the perfect family and wonderful children was not what he was seeing. He was completely devastated, and my usual 'knight in shining armour' needed rescuing himself.

I was also disappointed that my husband was not as close to God as I wanted. He would not go to

God's presence as I had always asked, but was content with the regular prayers we made together within the home. I felt that if my husband had a close relationship with God as the head of our home, maybe he would pray, and everything would be fine. I thought that maybe God was seeking my husband and was therefore withholding our healing until that happens.

All these were going through my mind and giving the devil a foothold to breed contempt. God, in His mercy, showed me that I needed to get closer to Him first and remove my focus from apportioning blame. The bible says in Acts 16:31," Believe in the Lord Jesus, and you will be saved, you and your household". Therefore, as I continue to seek the Lord, I will be empowered to intercede on behalf of my family until they all come to the saving knowledge of God.

My mother was next in line. My mother is my spiritual head and a strong source of strength in difficult situations. So naturally, I turned to her for guidance and support. I would constantly call her and narrate the difficulties we were facing as they arose. As usual, we would pray together and continue to believe that things would change for the better. However, unknown to me, every time I called my mother, she was filled with sadness and would go to God crying and lamenting about my situation. My mother would often present a strong front, but the difficulties with my children were seriously bothering her.

One day, she went in to cry to God as usual, and God told her to ask me to come to Him instead. That I should no longer narrate the children's difficulties to her anymore, but to Him. When my mother said this, I felt abandoned. I felt that the most important people who should hold my hand through this storm had abandoned me. Who do I then speak to about these challenges with my children?

I could not talk to my husband because he was struggling to manage it all, and now, I could not talk to my mother either. I felt angry, disappointed, and hurt. However, this exposed how dependent I was on my mother's ability to pray to God and provide solutions. It showed that instead of going to God directly, I was using my mother as a middleman between me and God. This was because, in my heart, I knew that I was not close enough to hear God for myself, but my mother could.

The bible says in Matthew 6:8, "Your Father knows what you need before you ask him." Therefore,

God knew that I needed to focus on Him and learn to trust Him for myself instead of trusting in others to hear Him for me. We do not know when we build idols in our hearts by placing things or people where God should be placed in our hearts. For some, their trust is in the image and reputation that they have built for themselves.

This is contrary to the life of Jesus who we are called to emulate, "who made himself of no reputation", some translations said 'emptied himself' and took the form of a servant (Philippians 2 verse 5 -8). Meaning that nothing about his person mattered above the will of God. God sees our hearts and knows when we falsely claim that we trust Him. Our actions, rather than our words, often reveal where our trust truly lies. For some, it is total dependence on their jobs for provision, and when such people lose their jobs, some fall into depression or commit suicide, among other things.

This is what happens when we put our hope in created things instead of trusting in the Creator. God has told us in the bible to not be anxious about our life or our needs because He knows we have them and will provide what we need as we seek Him first (Matthew 6 verse 21 - 33). May God continue to open the eyes of our understanding in Jesus' name, Amen!

God continued the work of weaning me from dependence on others. Next was family and friends. I am blessed with a wonderful family who knows the Lord and, therefore, can pray with and for you when needed. My in-laws are also kind and understanding. However, no one could truly understand what we were going through. At the time, none of my family members had experienced such delays and difficulties with their children.

Most of my family were back home in Nigeria and could not understand what was going on. It seemed that God purposely isolated us during these years so that He could complete His work of teaching me to learn to trust Him. This was also the case with friendships. All my close friends were in Nigeria, and I struggled to connect with people due to our children's difficulties. We could not attend the majority of the ceremonies we were invited to because we had to make sure it was suitable for our children. Bearing in mind that our second son had been fed with a tube for many years, we had to consider many things before going out. This resulted in us being more isolated because we could not go to many places, and honestly, people could not understand what was happening with us.

By this time, the scriptures Proverbs 3:5-6. which states, "Trust in the Lord with all your heart and lean not on your own understanding, in all your ways submit to him, and he will make your paths straight." And, Jeremiah 17:5, "Cursed is the one who trusts in man, who depends on flesh for his strength and whose heart turns away from the Lord" became clearer. I began to draw closer to God. The people I had trusted to find solutions and help me through this trying time were not able to help.

The systems I looked up to for solutions seemed to be making it worse. I had no other option but to draw closer to my heavenly Father. Just as in the story of the prodigal son, my heavenly Father was running toward me. He had patiently been waiting for me to realise that He is the most important factor in my life. As I spent more time reading the bible and spending time in His presence, our intimacy grew. I could hear Him more often and more clearly. I had always wanted to hear His voice clearly, but we cannot effectively hear Him if we are far away from Him, both physically in terms of not spending enough time in His presence and spiritually when we have idols in our hearts. "Idols" in this case, simply means other things taking the place of God in our hearts. I thought my heart was fully His at this point, but God, who can search our hearts, had not finished with me yet.

I had to release my children to Him, too. This felt like the hardest of them all. God had to test my trust and obedience to Him. With all the difficulties we have been experiencing with our children, my love and protectiveness over them grew. I felt like I had to protect them with everything and from everything due to their vulnerabilities. I knew what they wanted before they asked and would do anything to ensure that they were ok. This was our normal routine for many years until God directed us to take them back to our country, Nigeria.

We had been praying for God's guidance and direction regarding our children for years. I have had dreams where God showed that He was making a way for us, but I never imagined that it would be this way. I had felt that any time we visit home, it would be for holidays and we would all return to the UK afterwards. However, this time we were to take our children home, get them settled in a good school in Nigeria and leave them with our family. I initially disagreed. I felt that it could not be

God's direction. Before this time, my children had never stayed overnight in a relative's or friend's house without either me or my husband, and now I am supposed to leave them in another country? I struggled with this for a while; however, God confirmed in many ways that this was His direction for us.

The story of Abraham and Isaac started to hit home. I began to imagine the emotions that must have gone through Abraham's mind following God's instruction to him about sacrificing Isaac. Sometimes we do not fully appreciate these stories until we begin to pass through similar situations that require us to surrender all to God and trust Him. I could write a whole chapter about how difficult this decision was for me, and the chapter would not be enough to contain it all.

God needed to make sure that I am completely yielded to Him in everything. That I would obey Him regardless of my feelings. It was not an easy path to take, but God is the author and finisher of our faith and knows the end from the beginning. Who better should I trust? My children are where He needs them to be, and that is what is most important, that we are in His will. Although I have not seen the full manifestation of all His promises on my children yet "I remain confident of this, that I will see the goodness of the Lord in the land of the living (Psalm 28 verse 13)" And "I will hold fast the profession of my faith without wavering; for He that promised is faithful and trustworthy (Hebrews 10 verse 23)".

Chapter 5

The most important decision

The main purpose of writing this book is to highlight the most important decision we as humans can make in this life. Daily, we are faced with countless things to accomplish and decisions to make, but some of us miss the most important one. The bible says in Matthew 16:26, "For what is a man profited, if he shall gain the whole world, and lose his own soul?". Some of us are focused so much on what is happening in the physical realm and trust in our intellectual ability to carry us through life.

But if we pause for a moment to consider a few questions. Why are we here? How did the world truly come about? What do you believe about the existence of God? We need to sincerely consider these things and tell ourselves the truth about what we truly believe. I read a book once about a Muslim woman who was given a bible and decided to read it out of curiosity. After reading some parts of the bible, she prayed an innocent and sincere prayer, asking God that if He truly existed, to please reveal Himself to her. That was all the invitation our heavenly father needed, and that was how their journey began.

Often, we are not honest even to ourselves about our true beliefs. It is better to decide for yourself whether you choose God or the way of the world. We cannot be in the middle because there is no middle ground. In Revelation 3:16, the bible says, "So, because you are lukewarm—neither hot nor cold—I am about to spit you out of my mouth." That verse shows us how much God detests people who are lukewarm. We cannot claim to be Christians, and there is no difference between us and the world. That is not true Christianity.

Therefore, the first decision is to choose who you will serve, God or the god of this world. I truly hope you choose to walk with Christ because there is no better choice on this earth. No human will love, understand, protect, and guide you through this journey of life like our heavenly Father. It is the singular most important decision in life. If you have made this decision to walk with God, I am so excited for you. If this is your first time acknowledging this or you are not sure if you are still right with God and would like to rededicate your life to Him, please pray this prayer with me below –

Heavenly Father, I thank you for today. I have decided to follow you all the days of my life. I believe in your son Jesus Christ, that He lived and died for my sins and on the third day, He arose. I decree that Jesus is my lord and personal Saviour. I invite you, lord, please come into my life and take over in Jesus' name, Amen!

As you pray this, believe in your heart that you have received Him and it is done. Congratulations!

This singular decision changed my life and has been my saving grace through life's storms. Without God, I do not know how my family and I would have coped these past years. You may say that maybe God is there to lead us only through difficult times. But that is not true. God wants us to come to Him with everything - our plans, wishes, experiences, questions, and thoughts (Proverbs 16:3; Psalm 37:5). I have experienced God's guidance in many areas of my life. One of the areas was my second degree and how I secured a job soon after.

I had wanted to study nursing or midwifery years ago, and I attempted to pursue this but was not successful. As I learnt to seek God more, I started asking Him to direct me regarding what course to study and which university to attend in the UK. At that time, He revealed that I needed to support my brother and that it was not yet the right time. So, I put the idea on hold. Years later, I brought it back to God, and it was the right time. He had led us to move to our new home, which is close to a university. I was able to study part-time, just as I had always wished. He guided me throughout my studies, and despite the stresses and challenges, I achieved amazing results.

After my graduation, I started praying about where to work. As I presented it to God, I started to complete job applications. Initially I was receiving negative responses from the applications. Then, unexpectedly, God prompted me to prepare for interviews, even though I had not received any invitations yet. Trusting His lead, I began my preparations. A few weeks later, I received an invitation to an interview. The questions were mainly those I had studied for, and I ended up getting the job—again, it was close to home and part-time, just as I had wanted.

Our Lord delights in guiding and directing us through life if we ask Him to. Inviting Him to guide us is not when we make plans and ask Him to bless them. That is self-will. The Lord wants to be involved from the start. We should present what we are looking to do and ask if it is His will. From there, we ask Him to guide us to what He wants us to do and move according to His direction, not our own will or plans. That way, we are sure that we are in His will.

A few things I have learnt on this journey so far -

Until you choose God and begin to learn His ways through the study of the bible, you will not understand the extent of His love for us. God gave Jesus Christ to die on the cross for us, not because He was sure that we would come to the saving knowledge of Him, bearing in mind that He gave us the will to choose. However, He loves us so much that He gave Christ on a 'MAYBE' that we would choose Him. It astounds me the depth of His love, which we would not fully understand on this earth. His love assures me that He, who gave Christ while I was a sinner, will not withhold anything good from His own.

We might think that our circumstances are beyond repair or that we are too "messed up" for God to love us. Those are all lies from the enemy. Due to my family circumstances, I had wondered how God could change things in my life. Even to write this book, which He had talked about a few years ago. When He said it, like Sarah in the bible, I laughed in my mind because I was too busy with my children and life. I thought it was impossible to ever have the time to write, but I accepted. Unknown to me, the master planner was orchestrating things in the background to ensure that He provides me the means and ability to do what He has called me to do. Do not worry about your circumstances, just come to Him.

It is also this love of God that makes Him not impose Himself on us until we have come to the end of ourselves and seek Him. The bible says in Revelation 3:20, "Behold, I stand at the door and knock. If anyone hears my voice and opens the door, I will come in to him and eat with him, and he with me." The Lord will not barge into your life without invitation. Often, people have said that if God is all-powerful, why then would He not force people to do His will instead of watching the evil that is prevalent in the world? I ask, what is love without choice? How can you say that someone truly loves you if they cannot choose to love you? God does not want robots. He will create opportunities for us to encounter Him and leave us with the decision to either choose Him or not.

Often, when things are going well in our lives, we tend to believe that our successes are solely due to our own efforts. This mindset can lead to pride and vainglory. The Lord reminds us that He opposes the proud (James 4:6), which is a concerning position to be in. Unfortunately, many people walk around feeling successful, unaware that they may have been given over to their own desires (Romans 1:24, 26, & 28). To society, these individuals may appear "blessed" and prosperous. We must be cautious when we rely on our own will instead of seeking God's guidance. Sometimes, it is His mercy that introduces unfavourable circumstances to encourage us to pause and seek Him. He is always near, waiting for us to turn to Him in every situation. God desires to lead us because He knows the end from the beginning; He is the Alpha and the Omega.

Another thing I have learnt is that God desires to commune with us. Just as parents enjoy spending time with their children, our heavenly Father loves to spend time with us. You cannot get to know someone unless you spend enough time with them. The process of becoming close friends involves spending dedicated time together to build familiarity and trust, allowing both individuals to determine if they share a compatible connection worthy of a close friendship. Same way it is when getting to know our Lord. We need to make out time daily to spend with God. Create a time every day to spend in a quiet place, reading about Him – that is, reading your bible/other Christian books that would help you grow your knowledge of God, worshipping and praying to Him. When we have decided what time to come to His presence, it is important to invite the Holy Spirit to come in and dwell with us during this time.

I have found that what often hinders this flow of communion is our need to focus on ourselves and our present desires. We often come to God when we need things. This is not necessarily bad, but we should not limit our communion with our Father to asking for things. He wants a relationship! How would you feel as a father or mother when your children only come to you for things? You would want to know how everything is going in their lives, and would like them to inquire about things happening in your life too. Therefore, as we have needs, so does our heavenly Father have His will and desire, which He wishes to see accomplished on the earth. Remember our Lord's prayer? "Thy will be done on earth as it is in heaven" Our Father wishes to partner with us so that His agenda will come to pass on earth. As we spend time in His presence, we will learn more about Him and His ways. When we pray and seek His face, we ought to ask Him what He desires us to do for Him. I have learnt to ask God to align my will and desires with His so that I will desire what He desires for me.

Chapter 6

More things I have learnt over the years

I now understand that prayer is communication between us and God. Therefore, we should expect to hear from God when we pray. Some people may ask, Does God speak? Yes, He does. God speaks to us through dreams (Job 33:14-18, Acts 2:17, Numbers 12:6, Matthew 1:20, Acts 16:9, Matthew 2:12-13,24, etc). God desires to speak to His children, and in our busyness, it can be difficult for us to quieten our minds to hear Him. Therefore, while we sleep, our minds are quietened enough for Him to bring us answers to prayers, visions, warnings, and guidance/direction.

It is important to write our dreams down immediately we wake up so that we do not forget the message we have received from God. Some books have discussed this means of communion with God explicitly, such books include Spiritual colours and their meanings in Holy Ghost school by LaFAMCALL Ministries and The Power of your dreams by Stephanie Ike Okafor.

Another way that the Lord speaks to us, although He does not often use this method, is through an audible voice. He showed this with Moses and the Israelites in Mount Horeb (Deuteronomy 4:12), Paul's conversion on his way to Damascus (Act 9:3-6), Jesus' baptism (Matthew 3:17). Another way He speaks is through the holy spirit within us (Romans 8:16). As children of God, we have the holy spirit in us guiding and leading us into all truth (John 16:13).

We should therefore be expectant when we pray to hear our heavenly father speak back to us. If you are struggling to hear God, pray and ask that His voice would be clear to you according to His word, which says that "my sheep hear my voice and I know them" (John 10:27). This is the advantage we have as children of God. To be guided through life by the creator of the heavens and the earth, to be led by the only one who knows the end from the beginning. The bible says in Jeremiah 33:3, " 'Call to me and I will answer you. I will tell you marvellous and wondrous things that you could never figure out on your own". Therefore, tap into this today so that God will begin to lead you.

The manner of prayers we make often show where we truly are on this journey with Christ. It is good to know that the Lord would provide for our material needs as the bible says in Matthew 6 verse 25 – 34, Philippians 4:19. However, in 1 John 5:14-15, the bible says, "And this is the confidence that we have toward Him, that if we ask anything according to His will, He hears us. And if we know that He hears us in whatever we ask, we know that we have the requests that we have asked of Him." This shows that God wants us to ask according to His will. You may ask, what is His will? The Lord can speak to us directly about what he wishes to see accomplished in and through us.

The bible is also clear about many things that the Lord wills. For instance, God wants everyone to be saved – 1 Timothy 2:4, 2 Peter 3:9, John 17:3. Therefore, when we say prayers that focus on people's salvation, the Lord is glad to answer. The Lord also wants His children to overcome the flesh and live according to the spirit – Romans 8 verse 12-13, Galatians 5 verse 16, Romans 8 verse 5-8. Living according to the flesh is yielding to the desires of our flesh. It does not necessarily always mean sin, but it can also mean things or activities that hinder and distract us from getting closer to God.

Personally, after praying for God to align my will with His, I began to see it manifest in my life in many ways. One of the ways is that I am yearning more for Him and seeking ways to learn and grow in my knowledge of Him. For many years, I enjoyed watching lots of movies and can watch movies for hours when I get the opportunity. It was one of my favourite things to do. For some time now, the desire to watch movies has reduced drastically, and although I still watch movies at times, I do not derive much pleasure from it anymore. Instead, I find myself listening to the word of God online whenever I can throughout the day.

When I discuss with my close friends, it is about God. This is not to say that it is wrong to watch movies, but that God has removed that appetite, so that something that does not necessarily bring me closer to Him has been replaced by a desire to do that which draws me closer to Him. For any individual who struggles with addictions in their life, which they may have tried to stop but are not able to, ask the Lord. The bible says in Philippians 2:13, "For it is God who works in you, both to will and to work for His good pleasure." It is He who does the work in and through us. Therefore, begin to pray in alignment with His will and watch how your life will be transformed for His glory.

Another thing I am learning is that as a Father, God expects us not to remain baby Christians forever. He desires for us to continue to grow in Him, and our growth and maturity in Christ is a continuous journey which accelerates through divine knowledge. The more we know Him, the more divine light shines in the areas of our ignorance and darkness. Therefore, let us continuously feed our spirit man with the word of God. Thankfully, there are many versions of the bible available now. Pick whichever you prefer and make a habit of reading your bible daily.

We need to read, study, and continually meditate on the word of God. As you read, ask the holy spirit to open it up to you. You will be amazed as you learn more about God and grow in intimacy with Him. Instead of scrolling on social media for hours, listen to the word of God online. Ask the holy spirit to lead you to the right preachers to listen to, because not every preacher online is sent by God.

We need to ensure that we are attuned to God all day by keeping our environment saturated with the presence of God. Listen to praise and worship songs and keep the right circle of friends. The people we surround ourselves with influence us. Therefore, if there are close friendships that do not draw you closer to God, it may be time to end those friendships; otherwise, they will act as a snare on your journey with Christ.

What we watch, listen to, and discuss influences what we think; as Proverbs 23:7 says, "as a man thinketh in his heart, so is he". It is immensely important that we guard the gates through which the world can infiltrate and influence us. Let us remember our charge in Philippians 4:8, which says, "Finally, brothers and sisters, whatever is true, whatever is noble, whatever is right, whatever is pure, whatever is lovely, whatever is admirable—if anything is excellent or praiseworthy—think about such things".

This is a charge to be intentional about what we focus on. We cannot minimise issues and say that it does not matter because it does. There is something I heard a preacher say that, "the devil we are playing with is not playing with us". This is very true, because the devil is intentional in ensuring that our environment and world are filled with distractions everywhere. Therefore, let us be mindful of what we hear, watch, think and entertain. Ask the holy spirit to remove the desires that are not of Him from you, and He will do so.

I have also come to realise that we are all sent by God into this earth for a reason and a purpose. The bible says in Jeremiah 1:5, "Before I formed you in the womb, I knew you; before you were born, I sanctified you; I appointed you as a prophet to the nations". We are sanctified! We are prophets! However, we do not always realise this because we are not all standing in front of a pulpit. Yes, we are not all called to the pulpit, but we are all sent by God into this world.

I believe that each of us has an assignment to fulfil in Christ. Jesus came to the world to fulfil the purpose of making a way for humanity's redemption. Therefore, God has seen the needs of our present time and decided to send us as solutions and light to the world. You can be the solution God sent to restore the health sector in your community, or resolve the issues with electricity. God sees a need and sends man. Your role might be to accelerate the use of tech for the kingdom of God or advise government and organisations towards embracing policies that support the heavenly agenda.

Our lives have more meaning than we can understand. We are not sent just to seek a thriving career, build a wonderful family, and amass wealth and influence for ourselves and our families. These in themselves are not wrong, but that is not our purpose. The bible says in Matthew 6:33, "But seek first His kingdom and His righteousness, and all these things will be given to you as well.". When we seek to know God first for ourselves, not seeking a third party to act as a middleman between us and God, we grow in intimacy and maturity in Him. As His word says, he would add every other thing that we need to complete our assignment to us. Therefore, when the wonderful family comes, you will understand God's purpose for the family and your role in raising the godly seeds He sends you. When the finances come, you understand that you are not a reservoir, but you are meant to let the resources flow to finance God's agenda as He directs.

Furthermore, I believe that we are called to community. Jesus, during His walk on earth, had 12 disciples. I believe that we are all called to walk this journey with others so that we can encourage and sharpen one another along the way. The bible says in Ecclesiastes 4:9-10, "Two are better than one, because they have a good reward for their toil. For if they fall, one will lift his fellow. But woe to him who is alone when he falls and has not another to lift him!" Therefore, think about your life. Do you have people or someone in your life who you can be vulnerable around? Who can speak truth and life into you freely without fear of offence and misunderstanding?

When I recently arrived in the UK, I did not have close friends who I felt were aligned with my values. I began to pray for God to send me someone or people to walk with me. By His mercies, He connected me to someone who has been like a sister for over a decade, and now I have a community in the UK by His grace. Thank God for communication systems that have made it easy to speak with people all over the world. However, if you feel like you do not have destiny friendships in your life, ask the Lord to connect you with those He has destined you to walk with in this season and trust as He leads you to them.

Finally, God is a consuming fire. Most times, we forget that as well as the lamb, Christ is also the Lion. We often treat God as if He were human and on the same level as we are. He is God! The creator of heaven and earth, who should be approached with awe and reverence. He loves to relate to us with love and kindness, but we must never forget that He is the almighty God. He operates in laws and principles which we must abide by as His children. We might fall off at times, but we need to understand that there are wages for sin. He will not, due to His love, shield us from experiencing the consequences of our sin. Remember the story of David and Bathsheba in the bible? David paid for the sin he committed when he killed Uriah so that he could have his wife. Although the bible calls David the man after God's own heart, he still had to face the repercussions of his sins. That is our God.

The bible says in Ecclesiastes 10:8, "Whoso breaketh an hedge, a serpent shall bite him". That is part of God's principle. He will protect us so long as we do not disregard the boundaries of our consecration in Him. Otherwise, if we step out in ignorance, disobedience, pride, or rebellion, we bear the consequences of whatever happens to us. It is therefore important that if we notice that we have mis-stepped or fallen short of His glory, we must quickly come to Him in true repentance for His forgiveness. Just as the bible says in 1 John 1:9, "If we confess our sins, He is faithful and just to forgive us our sins and to cleanse us from all unrighteousness."

I pray that our Father, the Almighty God, who is able to keep us from stumbling and present us without fault before His glorious presence, will continue to lead us to fulfil His perfect will on earth as it is in heaven, in the mighty name of Jesus, Amen! God bless you!

Printed in Dunstable, United Kingdom